VIEW EAST FROM THE
BROMLEY - 83RD AND
BROADWAY - APRIL 23, 1987
ROBERT MILES PARKER

THE UPPER WEST SIDE / NEW YORK

STANDING ON BROADWAY
JUST LOOKING AT
THE OLD PEOPLE – THINKING
ABOUT, LIKE THEM,
ALL I'VE GONE THROUGH
THIS YEAR.

RMP
10-15-87

THE DORILTON
171 West 71st Street at Broadway

When the Dorilton was built by Janes & Leo in 1900, architects and critics jeered; now it is one of the most beloved buildings on the Upper West Side. A looming crumble of muscled ladies and decorative frosting, it shouts out that the West Side was meant to be Paris, New York style. The Dorilton is the first and most audacious of the city's Beaux-Arts beasts.

ROBERT MILES PARKER

THE

Upper West Side

NEW YORK

LATE SUMMER
LADIES IN
RIVERSIDE PARK

HARRY N. ABRAMS, INC., PUBLISHERS, NEW YORK

To **DAVID**

who gave me New York

Ðavid in the kitchen
on West 73rd Street

EDITOR: Ann Whitman

DESIGNER: Barbara DuPree Knowles

Copyright © 1988 Robert Miles Parker

Published in 1988 by Harry N. Abrams, Incorporated, New York
All rights reserved. No part of the contents of this book may be reproduced without the written
permission of the publisher

A TIMES MIRROR COMPANY

Printed and bound in the United States

LIBRARY OF CONGRESS CATALOGING-IN-PUBLICATION DATA

Parker, Robert Miles.
The Upper West Side / Robert Miles Parker.

p. cm.

1. Architecture—New York (N.Y.)—Conservation and restoration. 2. New York (N.Y.)—
Buildings, structures, etc.—Conservation and restoration. 3. Upper West Side (New York, N.Y.)
—Buildings, structures, etc.—Conservation and restoration. 4. New York, (N.Y.)—
Description. 5. Upper West Side (New York, N.Y.)—Description. I. Title.
NA108.N72P37 1988
720′.9747′1—dc19   ISBN 0–8109–1747–5   88—6252

ACKNOWLEDGMENTS

Many of the people who shared their love of buildings did so anonymously, as they saw me drawing on the streets. I thank them all for their encouragement.

Others introduced themselves, took me into their homes and lives. This book wouldn't have happened had Pat Hetkin not found me drawing on 72nd Street, demanded to know who I was and what I was doing. She told me what preservation meetings to attend and who to meet—especially Arlene Simon, who has given her whole life to preserving the Upper West Side through her organization, Landmark West. Arlene and Jean Martowski always took time from their preservation work to help my more personal project, as did Tony Wood, who believed in me and became my friend.

At one of those endless meetings I met Barbara Harnick and showed her my work. When she heard of my idea—a document of the rapidly changing West Side—she immediately called Paul Gottlieb at Abrams, and my dream was realized. To Barbara, Paul, designers Barbara Knowles and Judith Michael, and to all the people at Abrams, including Julie DeMatteo and Toula Ballas, who listened on the phone and chattered their support, I would like to express my gratitude for helping to make my private vision a public document.

Longtime friends, like Carleton Knight and Tom Davis, offered as always their support and encouragement; I am only sorry they did not live to see the project completed. Charles Hasbrouck, in the brief time I knew him, gave unstintingly of his vast knowledge about the West Side. And Mosette Broderic, although I met her only at the end of the project, helped me formulate my own conclusions. I wish that I had had time to assimilate more of her information.

To Merika Gopaul, Ed Iwanakee, and other friends and collectors in San Diego and throughout the country, who suffered with me through this book as they have through the two earlier ones, any thanks I can offer will be insufficient. My only consolation is that they at least knew what they were getting into. For my new New York friends, who didn't know but bore with me anyway, I can only hope the result reflects the quality of our shared dream.

–R.M.P.

Katie-Dog has a New York dinner. Now she's a city dog, safe behind her triple locks.

VIEW WITH 411 WEST END AVENUE
Between 79th and 81st Streets

West End Avenue is not all stiff and flat, not always the wall people think it is. Sometimes it has quizzical curves, both old and not so old.

INTRODUCTION

I can remember a time when, as a visitor to New York, I would not think of coming to the West Side. It was dreary and scary; all my friends were either proper Villagers or even more proper East Siders.

I still had that attitude in 1985, when my friend and I decided to try living in the city. But the only place we could find to live was a sublet behind the Ansonia, so we moved to the Upper West Side.

The energy and variety of the place were immediately engrossing. We were stuffed into a left-over piece of a row house, with all kinds of people for neighbors: an elderly interracial couple, who had lived quite comfortably in their studio for over twenty years; a countertenor who practiced *Der Rosenkavalier* across the hall in the morning while I shaved; some Chinese violinists above us; and some Nigerians below. Out the windows, even more variety was to be found. Somewhere a soprano rehearsed *Tristan*; she was answered by a bass doing scales from someplace else.

And the streets! They were full of unusual characters—dancers stretching, actors muttering lines, "bag ladies" and stylish matrons, all kinds of people mixed together. I had come to New York from Southern California, and the assortment of people here— of all different races, nationalities, styles, professions, and persuasions— it was foreign and delightful to me. The weather, too, amazed me; we don't have much weather out West, don't like it. And the color. I had never heard anyone talk about New York light. But it's quite special, much sharper than in San Diego. Streets become sheets of colors, studded with silver-reflecting windows. With their dark shadows, the colors make a sparkling crazy-quilt; in haze or rain, a patina of muted grays.

LAURA, A WORKING GIRL
ON BROADWAY
6·19·87 ·R·M·P·

But the most exciting thing of all was the architecture. It mirrored the mad antics and styles of the people dashing around. Architecture of course always reflects the people who make it. But what I read in the buildings of the West Side was special: a boundless energy, a lack of interest in conformity, and a little bit of madness.

My way of drawing helped me understand the West Side and its people even better. I prefer to draw directly from life, with only a dip pen and pot of ink at my side. Without preliminary work in pencil, the ink blots and the splatter of the street just become part of the composition. Everything is recorded, from pigeon droppings to rain drops to jagged lines made when my arm was bumped by a rushing New Yorker. From 59th Street to 110th, from Central Park to the Hudson River I lugged around a black portfolio containing a folding aluminum lawn chair and various drawing boards (the board size dictated to a degree the look of a drawing); I was accompanied, in all but the worst weather, by my dog, Katie. On days when even I couldn't survive outdoors, I borrowed windows from friends, friends of friends, or restaurants.

The Upper West Side was built, I guess, in seriousness; but most of it makes me smile. There are peculiarly shaped towers, amusing carved faces, lovely rows of townhouses, and monumental apartment buildings. There are charming bits that bring tears: secret lanes, old bricks, stores that offer treasures from all over the world. And the buildings themselves are treasures—breathing, watching, feeling.

I have had the opportunity to love the city in the best way—a private one. It is not the theater or the galleries, the museums or the great stores, that I love; it is the street. I have been very happy wandering the West Side with the Katie-Dog, just sitting wherever something has caught my eye and drawing it. There are many more images from the 70s and 80s, the two places we have lived in New York, than from the other Upper West Side neighborhoods. Usually, when I planned to draw something far away, I'd be captured by things right in my own backyard. The more you look, the more you see.

The Upper West Side is like Manhattan's suburban world. It speaks of comfort, strength, security. But the Hansel-and-Gretel houses, the Flash Gordon apartments, the tenements on side streets, the sophisticated row houses, and even the trendy shops and flashy restaurants may not last. In fact, when the book was completed, places and events had already changed, making this collection a frozen moment in time. Landlords and developers are eager to give us newer and bigger buildings, and in so doing, may destroy much of this delicate fabric. Already the revival movie houses are gone, as are many of the actors, writers, and musicians. The Upper West Side is too expensive now. Laissez-faire economics, which created this great area in the first place, may finally destroy it. Programs are needed to keep rents within the range of those artists and intellectuals and ordinary people who made the Upper West Side what it is. Also needed is a method of protecting the built environment. This is still a pure place, maintaining much of its original feeling. But it won't be for long.

The best bet for preserving the Upper West Side is through regulations. New York's powerful land-marking ordinance should be used to protect the architectural environment. Many Upper West Side buildings are among those that people the world over think of as "New York." To fail to preserve this heritage, would be a blot on the history of the world's greatest city.

THE UPPER WEST SIDE / NEW YORK

I HAVE SLICKED BACK MY HAIR, ADDED A FEW DIAMONDS, DRESSED IN BLACK-AND RETURNED TO THE UPPER WEST SIDE.

DEPARTMENT OF PARKS AND RECREATION BUILDING
59th Street between Amsterdam and West End Avenue, looking north

At the Parks Department building, way down at the beginning of the Upper West Side, we get a taste of the fun that awaits us. This little building is right in the spirit of things: there's a gargoyle with a football and one with a bat; there's a basketball gargoyle, and one, I guess, playing soccer.

12 WEST END AVENUE
At 60th Street, looking southeast

The storage place is a survivor of the old Upper West Side—
or the first hint of the magic in store right up the street. Its neighbor, an
auto transmission repair shop, suggests a more plebeian but necessary world,
while rising up in the background is a towering threat to small-scale elegance.
This is a fairy-tale view of sorts, complete with distant ogre.

AMSTERDAM AVENUE
At 60th Street, looking northeast

Without protection, this is what much of the Upper West Side will soon look like. The crazy quilt of architectural styles and people will crumble under the onslaught of developers. The look-alike world of the suburbs will become the West Side's as well, only taller and bigger. Landmarking—and the protective onus it provides—may be the only salvation, because in New York a landmarked building may not be destroyed unless hardship is proven.

Labels visible in the illustration: DARVASH BALLET STUDIO · STEPS 60th CONTEMPORARY + CLASSICAL DANCE STUDIO · jon devlin's dancercise · STEPPING OUT BALL ROOM DANCE STUDIO · FRANK•ERIE DRINKS • FRIES • BURGERS · TaB · MARTINS · PINA COLADA · FROZEN YOGURT · PAPAYA

1845 BROADWAY
Between 60th and 61st Streets, looking west

Somehow this leftover with a '40s feel has managed to survive here, where fancy-dull new buildings have largely taken over. This survivor suggests a time when sailors hung out at the bar while hopeful hoofers practiced their art upstairs.

THE ANGRY MOBIL GAS STATION
West End Avenue between 61st and 63rd Streets, looking west

This gas station sits right where whiz-bang developer Donald Trump plans to erect the world's tallest building. The proposed project has met with a great deal of opposition, as the tower would cast a dark shadow over most of the Upper West Side. Better just to have a grumpy gas station.

"ANY CHANGE TO SPARE?"

THE WEST SIDE YMCA
5 West 63rd Street, between Central Park West and Broadway, looking north

Built in 1929 by architect Dwight Baum, the Y has been compared to an Italian Hill town. Surely it's a great community place, and worth a careful look. Towers, balconies, and parapets abound—a cluster of visual delights. Too bad they want to build a modern tower on top of it.

LIBERTY STORAGE WAREHOUSE
43 West 64th Street, between Central Park West and Columbus, looking north

Naturally, the Upper West Side has its *own* Statue of Liberty—a pleasant counterpoint to the seriousness of Lincoln Center across the street.

THE PRASADA
50 Central Park West at 65th Street

One of the great Central Park West apartment houses—built in 1907 by Charles W. Romeyn & Henry R. Wynne—the Prasada once had a drive carved out of the entrance so carriages could easily unload elegant passengers. The huge banded columns seem a great symbol of comfort, like money bunched together.

17

THE ARMORY

66th Street between Central Park West and Columbus, looking south

Every neighborhood needs a fortress for protection, and most New York neighborhoods have them. The Upper West Side's is a cardboard cut out castle from a child's toy box, designed in 1901 by Horgan & Slattery. The building is now host for Channel 7 and TV's oldest soap, "All My Children," but it could still use fancy-dressed, brass-buttoned guards to hold down the fort.

19

METROPOLITAN OPERA HOUSE
Lincoln Center between 66th Street and Columbus, looking west

I think this is the only interesting view of the Met—Wallace &
Harrison's 1966 concoction. Lincoln Center, started in the '60s, is credited
with the rebirth of the Upper West Side. But to my eye, the center looks
flat against the sky, with a truncated air. Like much of the new architecture
up here, the Met has nothing to do with what came before.

152 WEST 66TH STREET
Between Broadway and Amsterdam, looking south

A little Alamo church, in the desert of the Lincoln Center area.

THE VIEW FROM ARLENE AND BRUCE'S WINDOW
67th Street between Central Park West and Columbus, looking north

The views from 67th Street are particularly special, as most buildings near Central Park were designed by and for artists. Huge windows frame drawings waiting to be done. The Majestic, the Belvedere, the Beacon Tower, and the San Remo are the glories of this panorama.

VIEW WITH THE REGENCY THEATRE
67th Street and Broadway, looking northwest

The Upper West Side's last revival house has just closed, bought out by mega-movie showers who reflect the current vogue for more money and less art. Do not be lulled into acceptance by real butter on the popcorn—"elegant" moviegoing is here, just sleazy neon and an excuse for inflated ticket prices.

12–14 WEST 68TH STREET
Between Central Park West and Columbus, looking south

There's always a West Side rumor, and it's often related to the theater or films. Here's one: they say *Ghostbusters* was partially filmed here, in this once-upon-a-time townhouse (built in 1895 by Louis Thouvard). The day I drew two painted and bejeweled old ladies strolled out, looking for all the world like stars themselves.

Most New Yorkers eat out; cooking takes too much time for such busy, busy people. But Pat loves food.

SECOND CHURCH OF CHRIST, SCIENTIST
68th Street and Central Park West, looking southwest

This 1900 church by Frederick R. Comstock makes a fine contrast to the mostly mammoth apartment buildings that line Central Park West. It's not a churchy Gothic Revival piece —rather, the Second Church of Christ suggests classic Roman thought—an intellectual building reflecting the style of Christian Science.

THE VIEW FROM PAT'S KITCHEN
69th Street between Central Park West and Columbus, looking northwest

When you peer around Pat's kitchen wall,
you catch a West Side glimpse. Some people
don't have even this much of a view.

69TH STREET
Between Central Park West and Columbus

You know the kind of day when you're
so cross you can't think straight? This was one of
those days. Somehow an extra story grew on all the
buildings in this row!

28

190 COLUMBUS AVENUE
At 69th Street, looking Southwest

Sometimes I get tired of the Yuppies, the flashy merchants, and the overpriced restaurants of the "new-and-improved" Upper West Side. But then I think what the neighborhood was like before—an ugly part of town where visitors seldom went. And I think what fun it is walking along and window-shopping, or watching all the beautifully dressed festive people. The buildings are still here, protected by the success—and people are having fun. Maybe I'm just a Manhattagrump: Why should I keep the fun to myself? It's great on Columbus.

60, 62, AND 64 WEST 70TH STREET
Between Central Park West and Columbus, looking south

Down here you can hear opera drifting from the windows, sedate and sophisticated. Farther uptown, the sound is salsa, cheerfully blaring away.

A PRE-YUPPIE BUILDING
70th Street and Columbus Avenue

Can't you tell? There's no $100 sweatshirt store or trendy restaurant on the ground floor, just a service-oriented dry cleaner.

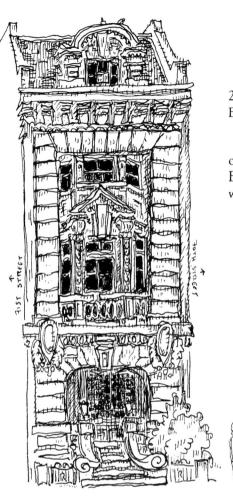

232 WEST END AVENUE
Between 71st and 72nd Streets

I have read that Louis-Philippe, once King of France, once lived near this Beaux-Arts structure. The Upper West Side was French in more than just architecture.

71ST STREET
Between West End and the Penn Yards, north and south

This block is one of the best-kept secrets of all. Two rows of candy-colored town houses sit comfortably and hope that Donald Trump doesn't ruin their secret by building the world's tallest skyscraper at the end of their street. Fall came early to the Upper West Side this year, and people are over their summer tension. Everything is gray and wet up at West End, shiny with red and green signal lights. More color in a city they call gray!

6–14 WEST 71ST STREET
Between Central Park West and Columbus, looking south

In this great jumble of stuff people will put up with the tiniest spaces, just to have New York.

GRACE AND ST. PAUL'S LUTHERAN CHURCH
71st Street between Central Park West and Columbus, looking north

Grace and St. Paul's snuggles into 71st Street so comfortably that most people pass it by—perhaps because it's been there longer than almost anything around. It's a Gothic brownstone building that invites the weary to stop for a minute —when the door is unlocked.

160 WEST 71ST STREET
At Broadway

The sort of building many West Siders call home. None of the glory of the great Central Park West apartments here, and none of the charms of the side streets. Yet this too is a community of people, happy in their houses.

GATEWAY TO THE UPPER WEST SIDE

72nd Street at Amsterdam and Broadway, looking north

The West Side really starts here; Broadway and the avenues south of 72nd Street have mostly been lost to clamoring new architecture. But this view proclaims the glories that still exist: the subway kiosk, the Ansonia, the Dorilton, and the Apple Bank for Savings. A jumble of a view that is special, fragile—and, perhaps, doomed.

WEBER'S

The Gateway to the Upper West Side

72ND STREET - AMSTERDAM - AND BROADWAY

Robt. Milo Parker. April 18, 1986

WEST 72ND STREET
From Columbus to Broadway and Broadway to West End

This is the greatest business cross street on the Upper West Side. It is a house of cards—old styles leaning precariously on new enterprise—and offers everything from lottery tickets to "dairy" at The Famous. But 72nd Street is fragile as well; and some preservationists believe that the Queen Anne, Richardsonian Romanesque, and other styles here have been ruined by the street-level stores. Not true—the stores and restaurants only add to the vibrancy. I hear that many leases are up, and on the south side of the street, merchants are preparing to move on. The great character of 72nd street is about to be altered.

THE DAKOTA
1 West 72nd Street, at Central Park West

The Dakota is one of the greatest buildings in New York and one of the oldest on the Upper West Side. Most people are familiar with the story of its name: designed in 1884 by Henry J. Hardenbergh and built by Edward Clark, with Singer Sewing machine money, the apartment building was situated so far from the center of things that cynics teased it was virtually in the Dakota territory. It is a haunting pile of greenish-brown brick and peaked roofs, attracting curious tourists and suggestive of whispered secrets. *Rosemary's Baby* was filmed there. John Lennon was murdered there. Lauren Bacall, Leonard Bernstein, Boris Karloff, Judy Holliday, Judy Garland, and Rex Reed have all lived there—so have Roberta Flack, Jack Palance, Fanny Hurst, Paul Gallico... I reckon the list never stops. There are stories of servants hidden in attic dormers, their employers long dead; stories of rooms sealed off in elegant apartments with ghosts on moonless nights. The Dakota is the soul of the Upper West Side— crumbly, strong, proud, daring to be outrageous in a post-modern world.

THE ALL-STATE CAFÉ
72nd Street between Broadway and West End, looking south

History never stops on the Upper West Side. The movie *Looking for Mr. Goodbar* is reputed to have been based on an incident that occurred at this very Gothic café.

HELP ME.

311 WEST 72ND STREET
At Riverside

Great turn-of-the-century buildings by Charles Gilbert mark the beginning of Riverside Drive at 72nd Street setting the stage for the glorious streetscapes ahead. These houses cry out to be landmarks and protected from "development."

72ND STREET
Between Columbus and Broadway, looking north

Choose any piece of 72nd Street—from Riverside Park to Central Park, from the architecture of Cass Gilbert to Henry J. Hardenbergh—it's all a visual delight. Moderne, Gothic, Neoclassical, all crammed together in one kaleidoscopic swirl.

72ND STREET KIOSK
Sherman Square, 72nd Street between Broadway and Amsterdam

The crowded subway station at 72nd and Broadway is the key to the Gateway. Though much too small to handle its daily traffic, this Neo-Dutch Colonial kiosk is still much loved. Its token booth is manned by unshakable sellers and surrounded by throngs of grumpy people wanting to go somewhere fast. There are always one or two people asking for a handout, and often a cop on watch. Downstairs, where the trains come and go, there's often a singer or guitarist to add to the confusion.

A PENNY TO
EAT PLEASE
AS I AM
HOMELESS
AND
HUNGRY

THE PERMA-NAIL PLACE
72nd Street and West End Avenue, looking northeast

This is one of the grander row houses of the Upper West Side—bigger because of its position at 72nd Street and West End Avenue. The corner location is probably the reason the conical tower is such a monster. Some might say that what's happened to the house is monstrous, too: a Perma-Nail salon—what would the original family say?

OUR FIRST HOUSE
251 West 73rd Street, between Broadway and West End

We took an illegal sublet and paid a lot of money—*not* to the landlord—for one room with a wall dropped down the middle so it could be called two. The building boasted a black countertenor, an Asian family, an interracial couple in their seventies, and some people from Africa. The house is emptying. When someone moves, the landlord leaves the apartment vacant, slated "for repairs." This technique, called warehousing, is partly responsible for the shortage of places to live.

A New Yorker's apartment is a very tiny, and private, affair. We managed to jumble up our 73rd Street sublet so much that it resembled the world out the window. Despite the jumble, it was a place to get away from the madness: the unrelenting street stops at the multi-bolted door.

DAVID'S VIEW
Amsterdam between 72nd and 73rd Streets, looking east

These twins overlook Verdi Square. From a
window seat in the Utopia—a favorite coffee shop—
we can see the parade of beautiful people framed
against the Ansonia and the Apple Bank.

45

Within the drawing: WHEN CLINTON MET BARNEY HE SAID "YOU ARE MY LITTLE GOYA" AND ACCORDING TO THE NEW YORK TIMES TODAY, CLINTON WILDER IS DEAD.... HE DIED ON VALENTINES DAY

ROBERT MILES PARKER
FEBRUARY 15, 1986
MANHATTAN

CLINTON WILDER MEMORIAL
251 West 73rd Street

This interior of our crowded former house on 73rd Street is a gift in memory of one of my oldest New York friends, the producer of Beckett and Albee.

THE ANSONIA
2108 Broadway, between 73rd and 74th Streets

This 1904 sand castle by Graves & Duboy, with its scooped out windows and bulbous towers, combines all the best features of architecture of the Upper West Side. Once there were chickens and goats on the roof, to insure fresh produce for tenants. There were also seals in the lobby pools—probably not a source of food. And over the years, many of the music world's most important figures have lived here: Enrico Caruso, Lily Pons, Flo Ziegfeld. Bette Midler got her start in the cellar, performing at the swimming-pool-turned-bathhouse. Even today the place echoes with the sounds of singers warming up, scales, piano players tinkling, violinists playing.

47

TWO VIEWS
From West 73rd Street, looking north

I could sit for hours watching this view—the famous Ansonia on one side, and layer on layer of city before me.

73RD STREET
Northeast corner of Columbus

The restaurants are charming to look at, and the buildings are fun. But the food can be mediocre and some West Siders have left Columbus because of the influx of Yuppies and the bridge-and-tunnel visitors.

310–312 WEST 73RD STREET
Between West End and Riverside Drive

Little rainy-day houses, built by Charles Pierrepont Gilbert in 1887, ride the coattails of elegance of the Drive—which once rivaled Fifth Avenue for style.

73RD STREET
Between Broadway and West End Avenue

Like many New Yorkers, we were eventually forced to leave our sublet and migrate farther uptown. On moving day, 73rd Street seemed to be saying good-bye.

THE VIEW FROM JOEY AND ADAM'S HOUSE
74th Street between Central Park West and Columbus, looking south

A very elegant row, indeed, built by Percy Griffith in 1904, on a street that looks a bit like Georgian London. These buildings are suave and cool—as are their tenants, a classy lot.

120 WEST 74TH STREET
Between Columbus and Amsterdam

On a street full of flamboyant
and eclectic houses, this one stands out.

303–315 WEST 74TH STREET
Between West End and Riverside, looking north

They never stop pleasing, these rows
of West Side houses. When I'm walking up
the avenue, they beckon to me, inviting me to
detour down their streets, to learn their
secrets.

VIEW WITH THE LAST WOUND-UP
74th Street and Columbus, looking southwest

The fun of pre-Yuppie Columbus was epitomized by The Last Wound-Up, an overcrowded store dedicated to wind-up toys. It is still a pilgrimage spot, if you really want to know this part of town—as is Mythology, a couple of blocks up the street, and the funkiest toy store of all, Sweet Asylum on Amsterdam.

Warming up the cold night: a fiddle and an accordion outside Andy's Deli.

AMSTERDAM AVENUE
Between 74th and 75th Streets, looking east

This avenue has always had a working-class feel. Even now, although it's fancier than it used to be, Amsterdam still lacks the sparkle of Columbus. But in a quiet way, the buildings of Amsterdam are treasures. Notice the townhouse on the right corner—it was designed by Hardenbergh, who also designed the Dakota.

Amsterdam is changing. Sleazy bookstores are now smart clothing shops. The bar on the corner is gone, as is the Istanbul. The antique store and the Candle Bar are lonely holdouts from another time.

VIEW FROM THE LAUNDROMAT
74th Street between Broadway and West End, looking north

I never finished this view from our laundromat: the clothes got dry too soon.

309–313 WEST 75TH STREET
Between West End and Riverside

Glance up any street from Riverside Drive and you'll be rewarded with a little glimpse of Europe.

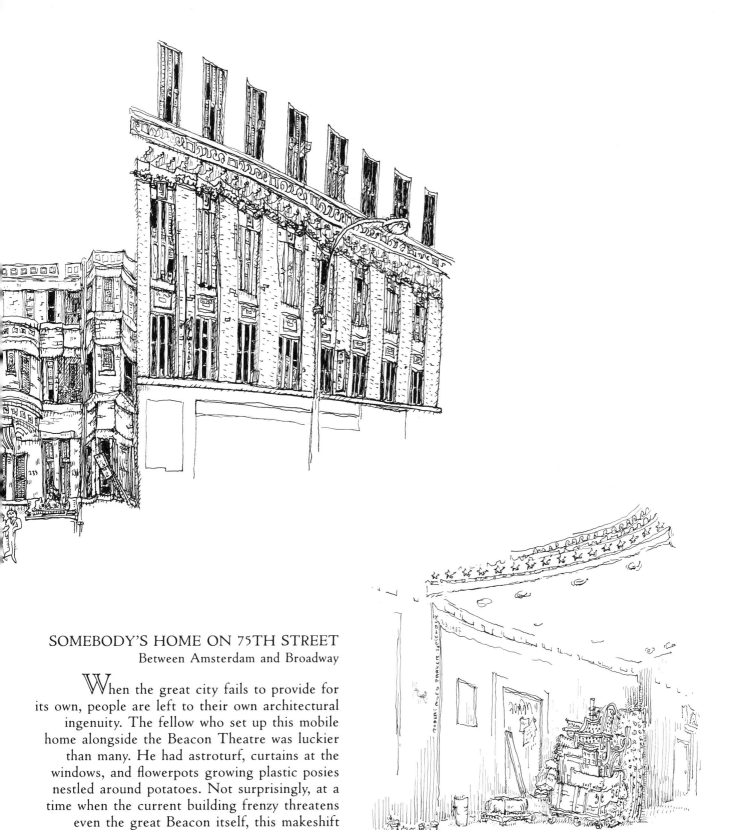

SOMEBODY'S HOME ON 75TH STREET
Between Amsterdam and Broadway

When the great city fails to provide for its own, people are left to their own architectural ingenuity. The fellow who set up this mobile home alongside the Beacon Theatre was luckier than many. He had astroturf, curtains at the windows, and flowerpots growing plastic posies nestled around potatoes. Not surprisingly, at a time when the current building frenzy threatens even the great Beacon itself, this makeshift dwelling lasted only a few days.

BROADWAY
Between 74th and 75th Streets, looking west

This has got to be the most special block
on the West Side. Jack LaLanne's over D'Agostino's,
Citarella's, and the Fairway. Colorful crowds of
people are forever pushing into the markets and
nagging or gawking at the absurd displays at
Citarella's Fish Market. (I have seen swordfish
surrounded by sea urchins, fish with bent cigarettes
dangling from their mouths, and flying fish dancing
with plastic Godzillas.) On this stretch of Broadway,
the "bag ladies" grumble, muscle-boys dash up to
the gym, and would-be stars dancercize at "Steps."

25 WEST 75TH STREET
Between Central Park West and Columbus, looking north

The 1880s produced small row houses; by the
1890s, the houses had grown larger and more exuberant
—like this one.

THE LA ROCHELLE, WHERE MEMPHIS IS
75th Street and Columbus

Originally, buildings on Columbus Avenue housed the working class; the El ran through and whisked workers downtown. La Rochelle was one of the best of the working-class houses with the main entrance on the side, away from the El's sparks and grime. Today, rents have soared beyond belief, and three businesses have recently left La Rochelle. But the very smart Memphis (so smart that it needs no sign)— remains.

59

THE VIEW WITH THE BIKE STOP BAR
75th Street between Broadway and West End, looking south

Right off Broadway, you can still find life as
it's always been: laundromat, barbershop, tarot-card
reader, and bar—businesses that have been around
forever. Customers and merchants alike mean to stay.
Overheard in the Bike bar: "We ain't letting them
Yuppies take over here, no sir!"

100–120 WEST 76TH STREET
Between Columbus and Amsterdam, looking south

As nice a row as one would want—
every visitor to the Upper West Side should
stop in the playground and look at 76th Street.
The architecture is not unusual, just pleasant,
and the playground opens the street wonderfully.
From the big tenement on the corner past the
boarded-up houses to the synagogue at the end, a
mighty fine view. On weekends, West Siders
gather in the playground's mammoth flea market,
to enjoy the treasures on both sides of the street.

WEST END AVENUE
Between 76th and 77th, east and west

Part of the Collegiate Historic District, these buildings can never be altered. These rows facing one another across West End Avenue stand as a monument to a time of individuality; the buildings boast small prizes—bats flying at corners, cupids holding window ledges. All of West End Avenue was once like this, so they say—the solemn apartment buildings we see today are second-generation.

COLUMBUS AVENUE
Between 75th and 76th Streets, looking east

It's not always as charming as it seems. Often cashiers yell at customers, waiters are indifferent, and sales clerks sullen. Rudeness is the norm: taxi drivers snarl angrily at old ladies in the crosswalks, and trucks try to beat the lights—sending pedestrians scurrying.

VIEW FROM PASTA AND DREAMS
West 76th Street at Broadway, northwest looking east

So perfect a view of the Upper West Side.
See them kicking up their heels at Jeff Martin's,
next door to the cathedral? Aerobics keep the
aspiring stars in shape and Broadway bouncing with
the sounds of disco. Next door to the Martin studio
are the Second Stage and the Promenade Theater
—important West Side drama centers, home
to Stephen Sondheim, Simon Gray, Tina Howe,
and performance artists Kathy and Mo, from
San Diego.

ANOTHER VIEW FROM PASTA AND DREAMS
West 76th Street at Broadway, from the northwest looking south

Somehow these buildings live with the seasons. In the spring and summer they bloom and smile; in the winter they are a haven from the cold. And in the fall, when everyone is scurrying around—happily doing "The Season"—the West Side's architecture bursts with autumn energy.

252 WEST 76TH STREET
Between Broadway and West End

A little French number that slid down from Broadway.

NEW YORK HISTORICAL SOCIETY
170 Central Park West, between 76th and 77th Streets

A Pompeian villa on Central Park West, and like an unearthed treasure house, it is full of wonderful secrets. Audubon's original watercolors are here, along with stunning collections of Gilbert Stuart and Asher B. Durand. Stuart's copy of the Washington portrait is here, as is Thomas Cole's series *The Course of Empire*, and some of Frederic Church's most beautiful landscapes.

WEST END COLLEGIATE CHURCH
77th Street and West End Avenue

Part of the Collegiate Historic District, this church was built in 1893 by Robert Gibson. The architecture recalls New York's Dutch heritage: stepped gables are like wooden shoes, clumping up the West Side skyline.

RIVERSIDE DRIVE
Between 76th and 77th Streets

In the late 1800s, Clarence True bought most of Riverside Drive from 72nd Street to 83rd; here he created rows of the most beloved castles in New York City. Slightly Dutch-looking, and a little bit comic in their self-conscious propriety, they are an integral part of the architectural fabric of New York. But why does one seem to see Snow White sweeping the walk, and little men darting around behind curved windows and peering from towers on high?

67

PYRAMID GARAGE
77th Street and Amsterdam Avenue

Built in 1891–94, the Pyramid Garage was originally the Mason Stables, with more than 150 stalls and space for 300 carriages. Horses stayed on the first two floors, and elevators lifted carriages to the upper levels. The stable was designed by Bradford Lee Gilbert in the popular Romanesque Revival style, and it is reported to have been more of a livery than a boarding stable. In 1915 the name was changed to Dakota, and the building converted to house automobiles. In the 1950s, Pyramid became the name. No one remembers when the Chirping Chicken moved in.

166, 168, AND 170 WEST 77TH STREET
Between Columbus and Amsterdam

The beloved stoops of the Upper West Side—or what's left of them—are an age-old Dutch tradition. In this part of 77th Street, the tradition, for the moment, lives on.

HOTEL BELLECLAIRE
77th Street and Broadway

Emery Roth's second Manhattan
building (1903) seems to be a cousin of the
Ansonia down the street. One could possibly
call it Beaux-Arts, but it's also full of Art
Nouveau pieces, and even some of the
simple lines of Viennese Secession. For the
pleasure of the passerby, there's a wealth of
materials—brick, wrought iron, terra-cotta,
and limestone. The Belleclaire has some of
the best decoration work on Broadway. Note
the Indian-like faces frowning at the traffic
and noise. The building itself has a noisy
feel, all those parts jostling to be seen.

THE AMERICAN MUSEUM OF NATURAL HISTORY
77th Street entrance, between Central Park West and Columbus

The West Side's storage closet, and New York's answer to the Smithsonian. And this is only one view. The earliest part of the museum is buried in bushes somewhere along Columbus, and the most imposing view—with memorial to Teddy Roosevelt—is on Central Park West. This Romanesque entrance, however, seems most appropriate for a place that houses effigies of monster elephants and snapping alligators, Indians rowing dugout canoes, and revealing South Seas sculptures. The museum is truly a never-ending pleasure, the perfect place for parents and children on a rainy Saturday.

78TH STREET
Between West End and Riverside

The heterogeneity of the West Side is reflected in its great row architecture. Each block is special, bursting with all sorts of people.

RIVERSIDE DRIVE
Between 77th and 78th Streets

Riverside Drive is a romantic place. Looking through the trees of Riverside Drive at the equally frilly buildings behind them, one recalls a lost European street.

VIEW FROM THE COPPER HATCH
78th and Amsterdam, northwest looking southeast

On our first evening on the Upper West Side, these buildings stood guard. We were eating at an outdoor café, and the Katie-Dog was tied to a nearby tree. On that warm August evening these buildings seemed to wait patiently to be drawn.

THE GUASTAVINO HOUSES

125–131 West 78th Street, between Columbus and Amsterdam

A displaced row of houses if ever there was one: these houses belong in Spain, and just looking at them makes you think of mantillas and castanets. No wonder—Rafael Guastavino, the architect, was a Spaniard, whose work enriched much of New York.

CORNER OF 78TH AND COLUMBUS. N.Y.C.
348 COLUMBUS · ROBERT MILES PARKER

NIGHT LIFE
78th Street and Columbus, looking northwest

This building, caught in the middle of the rebirth of Columbus, boasted a popular night spot for Yuppies. The clientele—loud, attractive—tend to ferret out trendy places in a flash. Their presence, sometimes, protects the architecture and infuses it with new life: they make the street prosperous.

The architecture hints at the hardworking Dutch burghers who settled Nieuw Amsterdam. Imagine what the avenue was like when it was lined with buildings like these.

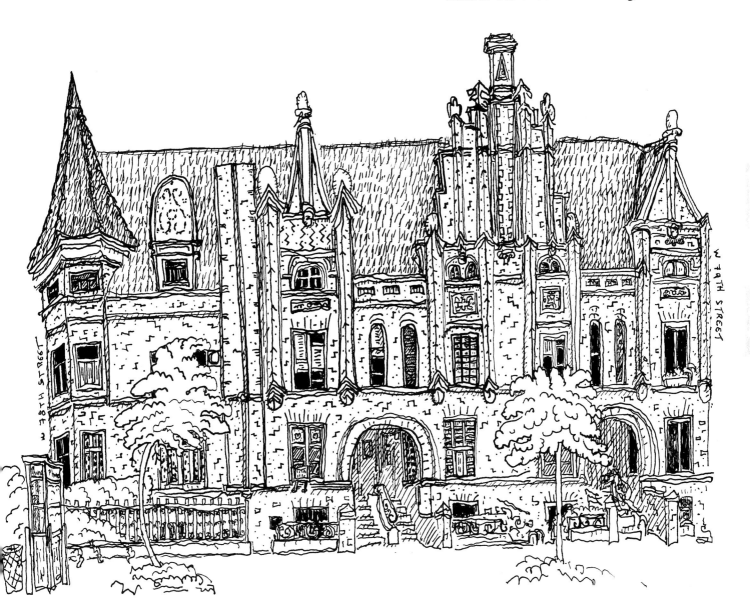

TWO VIEWS FROM SCOTT'S APARTMENT
79th between Columbus and Amsterdam

From a West 79th Street window.
A pleasant view, nothing special...

... Until you look again,
and the whole Upper West Side
opens up before you.

79TH STREET
Between Amsterdam and Broadway

A lovely Renaissance row, on the last street of the very beautiful people. From here on up, life gets more serious and people are more somber.

FIRST BAPTIST CHURCH
79th Street and Broadway

This inviting, eclectic 1892 edifice, designed by George Keisler, is
a symbol of the amazing variety of folk who call this neighborhood home.

80TH STREET
At Riverside Drive

Sometimes the city seems a fortress, an island of castles: workers come in from across the rivers, do their jobs, and go home at night. But the fairy-tale illusion is dispelled by the homeless. Here, across from these castles on Riverside Drive, a group of homeless people perch on the walls of Riverside Park to air their belongs and catch up on the day's doings.

CHARLES WAS BURRIED TO DAY (AND HE WANTED TO BE CREMATED)

202–204 WEST 80TH STREET
Between Amsterdam and Broadway

These buildings remind me of Dutch ladies wearing ropes of pearls and high lace collars. Dowagers, but proper, these Flemish dames.

80TH STREET
Between Columbus and Amsterdam

The tossing greenery of the trees
is a constant complement to a
West Side summer.

FROM ZABAR'S TO SHAKESPEARE & CO.
Broadway between 80th and 81st

Here's English village architecture overlain on Italianate.
Here, up the street, or at Pomander Walk, English was quite the
vogue in the early 1920s. And—speaking of vogues—there is
perhaps no place in all New York better known than Zabar's.
The glories of the deli and breads, the cooking accessories, and
the crowds are legendary; cars are parked three deep on Sundays.
I confess to an addiction to the chocolate croissants: I cannot walk
past without buying one or two—even on the way to the gym.

Thanks to the First Amendment, book peddlers don't need a license. This specialist sits outside Zabar's selling parts of the New York *Times*—a steal at 25¢ a section. On the Upper West Side, there are lots of ways to make a buck.

VIEW WITH SARABETH'S KITCHEN
Amsterdam Avenue at 80th Street

The old and the new in a Romanesque group. Amsterdam hasn't moved into the '80s quite so fast as Columbus, but it's on its way. McAleer's Pub and The Pet Bowl seem to be old friends. Sarabeth's pricey, pretty kitchen, an East Side import, has proudly joined in; a paisley eatery with a post-modern top.

COLUMBUS AVENUE
Between 80th and 81st Streets

Some of the less dressy Columbus cousins. Was the furniture store once a movie house?

MY SHOPPING CENTER
81st Street and Broadway

No shopping mall for me—
I'm a New Yorker now. I get lots
of my business done right on 81st
Street. There's a surprising, time-
less sensation evoked by visiting
the Chinese hand laundry in the
cellar, the printer next door, and
the dry cleaners upstairs over
the driving school.

81ST STREET
At Riverside Drive

Fairy-tale
architecture once
more.

81ST STREET
Between Columbus and Amsterdam

People stranger than the buildings
themselves emerge in the springtime, people
never before seen by their neighbors—
though they've been around for years.

THE BERESFORD
211 Central Park West between 81st and 82nd

The Beresford is one of Emery Roth's greatest buildings, and one of the most beloved castles on the West Side. Its three lanterned towers are beacons, emblematic of the picturesque grandeur found in no other part of town. This 1929 building is a blocky beast, a fortress-in-Spain, on the West Side.

VIEW ON AMSTERDAM
Between 81st and 82nd Streets, looking east

Most of the buildings along Columbus and Amsterdam are just tenements—not much to look at, the critics say. Not true. Notice the balance of chimneys on top, the end bays that nicely complete the structure. Note how the chimney lines slide down the façade—as pilasters—breaking the building into sections. And then that old story: change. Only La Gran Esquina, the barber shop, remains. La Conca Superette is now gone, and the other stores have been replaced by "smart" shops.

317–321 WEST 82ND STREET
Between West End and Riverside

Chimney pots, finials, and colonettes abound in this jumble of castles, c. 1892.

VIEW FROM LOUISA'S WINDOW IN THE SAXONY
82nd and Broadway, southwest looking east

When the snow starts to fall, people take cover in the restaurants on Broadway. On this street Marvin Gardens and The Front Porch, two neighborhood favorites, vie with the newer Song Thai restaurant, where martinis are served in sherbet glasses. Called "background buildings" for their supposedly boring character, they're full of interesting bits if you look closely. In the background, the towers of Holy Trinity and the omnipresent Beresford; I'm alarmed by the new thing that has gone up behind a beautiful old nickelodeon.

THE LIVINGSTON SCHOOL
82nd and West End Avenue

Before the big apartment buildings of the 1920s were built, West End Avenue was very Dutch. C.N.J. Snyder, New York's resident school architect, designed this building to reflect that heritage, with stepped gables and peaked dormers. This nice building was about to be destroyed—the school board planned a faceless high-rise condominium, where the school would lease some space on the lower levels. But Barbara Barrie and her friends started a battle that stopped the destruction.

THE WEST SIDE CLEANING CENTER
224 West 82nd, between Amsterdam and Broadway

Doing the laundry is never fun. But it's more interesting here than in a shopping mall —at least there's always a building to look at.

The Upper West Side—unique architecture, unique people. An Israeli art student covers the sidewalks with pastel reproductions of the Sistine ceiling, while passersby watch and toss money. Like Michelangelo (and like any good New Yorker), he writes his name and number across the work, in case someone wants a drawing on their sidewalk.

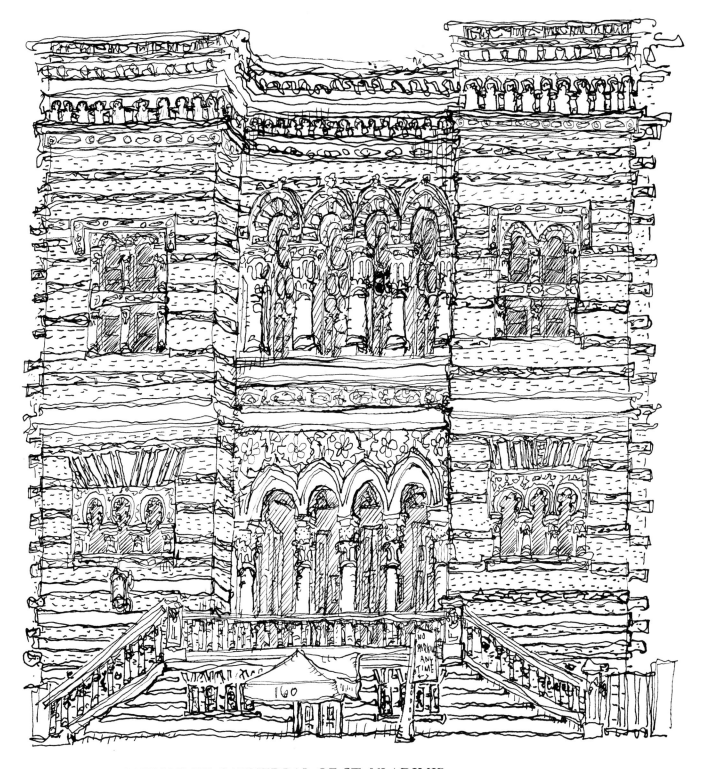

THE UKRAINIAN ORTHODOX CATHEDRAL OF ST. VLADIMIR
82nd Street between Columbus and Amsterdam

A fine contrast to a row of fine houses—and a great name for a church.

AMSTERDAM AVENUE
Between 82nd and 83rd Streets, looking west

The tenements of Amsterdam—a frozen piece of history. All the shops are intact, with no signs of the Yuppie intrusion in the guise of trendy shops. This block still offers used furniture, dusty antiques, luggage repair, and even an Irish bar. But it has changed since I drew it

This corner still seems to be a neighborhood: the old and lovable shops are still here, and Holy Trinity Church jumps out of 82nd Street.

94

THE LESLIE
83rd Street and Broadway

The Leslie is a good illustration of the West Side's problems—a "soft spot" waiting to melt. The second floor was reputedly once George Balanchine's studio. Now empty, the "largest studio space left in the city" gave way to changing times—a New York constant. Garlands and balconies will soon frame empty windows. The Plymouth clothing store and Chase Manhattan Bank have already moved. The others will follow. When this Red Apple is gone, the neighborhood will have no place to buy groceries.

BROADWAY

Between 82nd and 83rd Streets, looking east

These buildings make the city what it is; to walk past them is to be in New York. They are where the middle class lives comfortably, for better or worse; to buy in now you have to be rich indeed, but if you're already here, you can't afford to move. There is decoration at the top—lots of it. Architect Emery Roth always disguised his water towers as Romanesque houses, and fancied up the top floors to match. The lower stories are ornamented too.

THE KITCHEN WINDOW
West 83rd Street, looking east

In this compact life, a kitchen window can have shelves instead of curtains—making yet another storage space.

THE BROMLEY
Four views from the north, south, east, and west

The Upper West Side stretches away before you, full of a flavor and personality all its own.

THE AMIDON
233 83rd Street at Broadway

The Amidon is a building you might
never notice, unless you look up as you walk by.

LOOKING SOUTH FROM NANCY'S
110 Riverside at 83rd Street

Views of the Upper West Side from every window:
Nancy has a private roof garden in this view of the parapet
of the Clarence True castle across 83rd. Beyond lies the
whole island and even a glimpse of New Jersey.

LOOKING NORTH FROM NANCY'S KITCHEN WINDOW
110 Riverside Drive at 83rd Street

Out her kitchen window Nancy sees a glorious jumble of
buildings; each window peers back full of hidden adventures.
Sometimes I see a silent stranger pick up a coffee cup, take a sip,
and set the cup down again.

WEST END AVENUE
Between 81st and 83rd Streets

Just when you think you've seen a nice, sane New Yorker, he starts
twisting his mouth and talking to himself. Just when you think you're
drawing an ordinary apartment building, a gargoyle shows himself to you.

83RD STREET
Between West End and Riverside

We call 83rd Street home now. Home: an SRO (single-room occupancy) hotel, half-empty; our leftover row house; the dreadfully plain co-op; some early twentieth-century apartments; and the very elegant 110 Riverside. Truly a slice of the Upper West Side.

307 WEST 83RD STREET
Between West End and Riverside

This is now our home in the city—one room called two at $1200 a month. A fine tower of a building, it is the last piece of what was once a row. I'm especially fond of the seven lions at the top, standing guard.

307 WEST 83RD STREET
Interior view

Latecomers to the Upper West Side are forced to live the compact life. But no matter how tiny, home is home and a haven from the frenzy of the streets.

109 RIVERSIDE DRIVE
At 83rd Street

They say Gustav Mahler once lived in this castle designed by Clarence True. A nice thing to think about—whether the story is real or not.

In the fall, when Riverside Park changes to burnt oranges and yellows, I hear music; as the leaves fall on the high ground above the Hudson, Mahler is there.

TOM DAVIS MEMORIAL
Out the window on West 83rd, looking south

310-318 WEST 83RD STREET
Between West End and Riverside

Our 83rd Street view: a row of richly colored brownstones—perfect New York.

TEMPLE RODEPH SHOLOM
83rd Street between Central Park West and Columbus

Temple Rodeph Sholom moved up from the Lower East Side as members of its congregation assimilated into New York life; the synagogue, built in 1930 by Charles B. Meyers, is a grand, rich statement, a complex combination of Byzantine and Romanesque, Moorish and Gothic forms. The beautiful *shul,* or sanctuary, is enough to make anyone a believer.

ENGINE COMPANY NO. 74
83rd Street between Columbus and Amsterdam

How marvelous that this great city still uses a Victorian firehouse. This 1888 article by Napoleon LeBrun & Sons comes complete with dalmatian, boisterous bulky firemen, and large-eyed little boys getting in the way.

THREE VIEWS OF 84TH STREET
Between West End and Riverside

Looking south, from Kate's
window: A hazy November 1.

Looking north: A perfect
example of the timelessness that one
can find up here, with trees and row
houses comfortably sitting together.
The block association keeps everything
very clean (and they all let me draw
out their windows).

Looking east, from Liz's window. Edgar Allan Poe wrote "The Raven" on this street—two different houses claim the distinction—so 84th calls itself Poe Street and sponsors block parties, fairs, and carnivals in Poe's name. David, a Poe scholar, finds it odd to celebrate a writer so anti-social. But it's a good idea. In fast, anonymous New York, one needs such affairs to bring people together.

84TH STREET
Between Broadway and West End

As whimsical as
any buildings I've met on
the Upper West Side.

RIVERSIDE PARK
Near 83rd Street

Riverside Park is a very personal
place; Edgar Allan Poe, it is said, sat on
a rock here, and thought about things.
Perhaps because of the long, narrow shape
of the Park, each street feels the Park is
its own. Pleasant rambles, nice trees and
rocks, a wonderful feel and smell of the
river. The Park and Drive were designed
by Frederick Law Olmsted and Calvert
Vaux—who also designed Central Park.
It's rather nice to be surrounded by
magnificent landscaping.

RIVERSIDE
PARK AT 83RD ST
ROBERT MILES PARKER
SEPTEMBER 11, 1986

JIM THE MARXIST'S BOYHOOD HOME
125 Riverside Drive at 84th

The house looms ominously over the park, suggesting the most haunting of ghost stories. But our Irish friend who grew up there, with his nine brothers and sisters, tells of romping up and down halls and happily fighting in the streets. When his father died, his mother gave up the apartment because, though cheap, it was just more space than she needed!

BROADWAY FUNK
Between 84th and 85th Streets

They call this sort of row a "tax-payer" or "soft spot." I, for obvious reasons, call it "charming" and fear what the eventual replacement will be. We will surely lose Patzo's amusing bitten corner—appropriate for a restaurant, but not for a high-rise. Morris Bros. has itself just eaten up the World Health Center and gets to stay around longer. The vitamin store has moved farther uptown, beyond the limits of current fashion. The clever Morris Bros. has been around a long time and is staying in the game.

THE JUMBLED VIEW FROM HEATHER'S WINDOW
85th Street between Amsterdam and Broadway, looking north

Sometimes the West Side can be overwhelming!

85TH STREET
Between Central Park West and Columbus

Queen Anne citizens (c. 1885) all in a row, each different from its neighbors. I am always amused by the cameo portraits that appear, scattered about on various walls. They can be quite cheering on a dull day.

85TH STREET
And Central Park West

These townhouses are the only such buildings on Central Park West. From stoops to towers they make a fine silhouette, recalling a much easier, and more roomy, time.

THE BROCKHOLST
141 West 85th Street at Columbus

It's such a crumbly pile that the Brockholst remains one of the Upper West Side's best secrets. People just pass by, unseeing—and the building seems to just grow there. Those who do see the building surely miss its name—which is really only part of a vine.

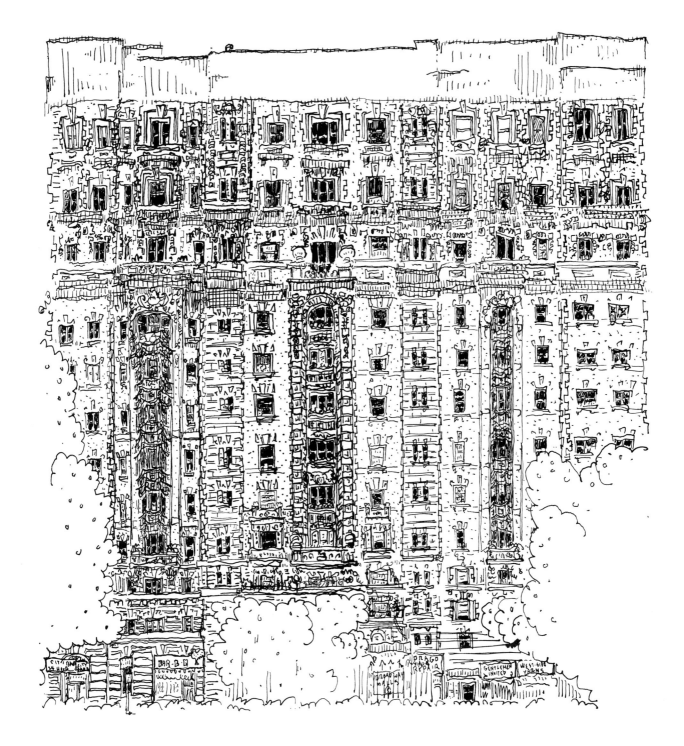

THE HOTEL BRETTON HALL
Broadway between 85th and 86th Streets

The Hotel Bretton Hall on shabby, busy Broadway reminds me of the old woman at the end of our street. She shuffles a few steps, rests her bag of groceries, then shuffles on, tattered but determined.

COLUMBUS AVENUE
Between 84th and 85th Streets

There are plenty of smart new shops
on Columbus—the quilt stores, restaurants,
and boutiques—but places like Tom's Pizzeria
are survivors from another era, lucky to be
able to cash in on the boom.

THE CASTLE
85th Street and West End Avenue

This is a castle that was saved:
an evil landlord had planned to build a
skyscraper over the top, but the forces of
good won the day. The strange townhouse,
perhaps Clarence True's last remaining
one, has unique door carvings—bats and
Southern vines. It will be permitted to stand
watch on the corner, where it's been lo these
hundred years.

118

VIEW FROM THE THREE STAR COFFEE SHOP
86th Street and Columbus Avenue, looking southwest

It's hard to believe that the El once ran up Columbus, carrying people to and from their jobs. What would the workers of the nineteenth century have thought of a shop for exotic cats and dogs?

103 WEST 86TH STREET
Between Columbus and Amsterdam

A wispy townhouse, almost alone on sophisticated 86th Street. Most of its neighbors are formidable apartments gone co-op, big and solid. Their strength makes this fellow stand out all the more.

VIEW FROM PHYLLIS'S WINDOW
160–164 West 86th Street between Columbus and Amsterdam

A frozen moment in the war over the West Side. Builders want to tear down and build higher; residents prefer the West Side as it is. A couple of people refuse to leave the center brownstone. If and when they do, the building may be demolished or added to—but either way, sunlight and air will be lost, as well as charm. In the meantime, the vacated buildings on each side wait like abandoned wrecks for the residents of the center one to give in.

VIEW FROM KEITH AND STACY'S WINDOW
86th Street between Broadway and West End

From their apartment, my friends kept tabs on the Red Apple executives (in their headquarters on 86th), or on the parking garage that used to store horses and carriages. No more, though—this is a lost view. Now there's a new high-rise in the way.

THE CHURCH OF ST. PAUL AND ST. ANDREW
86th Street and West End Avenue

R. H. Robertson's 1897 church has something for everyone, and turns every which way to be admired. The church once merged with another (now a synagogue) on 76th Street, thereby gaining a second saint. But all the saints in heaven won't help preserve this building, whose owners are fighting against a landmark designation.

THE MURDER INK BLOCK
87th Street between West End and Riverside

A close-up of the old view from Keith and Stacy's. This is a great block, from the restaurant where Isaac Bashevis Singer eats to the building that houses Murder Ink, the murder-mystery shop. Push the limp cats off the merchandise and discover an unparalleled collection of whodunits.

THE BACK OF THE BELNORD, FROM THE POPOVER
Amsterdam Avenue between 86th and 87th Streets

In the land of co-ops and condos, the Belnord is still a rental. The 1908 building, designed by H. Hobart Weekes, takes up a whole block and surrounds a courtyard—very Renaissance. This is a cold winter view, which was sometimes flaked with falling snow.

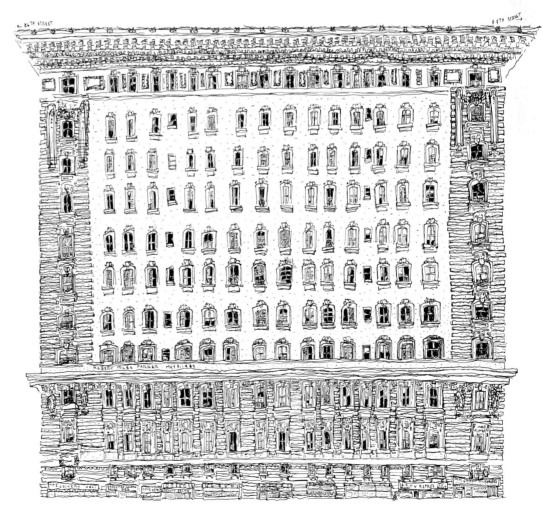

THE NORMANDY
140 Riverside Drive, between 86th and 87th Streets

I've often thought the Upper West Side can seem a bit like the suburbs: just a block or two from Broadway is a quiet, comfortable, unspoiled world. Emery Roth's Normandy (1939) is a perfect example of the solid comfort of that world.

VIEW WITH THE POPOVER
Amsterdam Avenue between 86th and 87th Streets

The Romanesque splendor of the West Park Presbyterian Church (built in 1890 by H. Hobart Kilburn) really stands out next to that tall apartment house. The church is famous for its involvement in community work. The first floor of the apartment building is the deli of the renowned Barney Greengrass, self-proclaimed Sturgeon King. Next door are taste treats from the friendly Popover Café.

303–311 WEST 87TH STREET
Between West End and Riverside

The West Side's row houses
never fail to delight, despite alterations
and intruding vines.

322–332 WEST 87TH STREET
Between West End and Riverside

When these side streets
are clad in spring green, the irksome
troubles of the day seem to fade.

THE SOUTH SIDE OF
WEST 87TH STREET
(300 BLOCK)
BETWEEN
WEST END AVENUE
AND RIVERSIDE DRIVE

THE VIEW FROM COLUMBUS GREEN
Columbus and 87th Street, looking southeast

The side streets are justly proud of their block spirit, which gives residents
a sense of identity within the context of the huge, anonymous city.

88TH STREET
Between Broadway and West End

The ever present garbage truck
servicing some charming brownstones.

FLOWER PEDDLER—
86TH AND WEST END

COLD JANUARY VIEW FROM DAVID'S WINDOW
88th Street between Central Park West and Columbus

A concerto of curves, bays, bows, and medallions: all these façades are like Vivaldi waiting for an audience.

89TH STREET
Between West End and Riverside

Fancy rooftops add a distinctive touch;
they are characteristic of the Upper West Side.
These have decorative stitching, like a bishop's cap.
It's too bad the front stoops are gone—where
can you sit and gossip with your neighbors?
Luckily, windows and fire escapes are still common.

CLAREMONT RIDING ACADEMY
89th Street between Columbus and Amsterdam

What a contrast: the properly habited
riders astride beautiful horses, trotting down tired
89th Street. This stable may be the only
one left in Manhattan.

603 AMSTERDAM AVENUE
Between 89th and 90th Streets

In the 1940s and '50s, the Upper West Side had a considerable Hispanic population. Now the march of gentrification is wiping out the Spanish and Puerto Rican flavor of the neighborhood; just a few bodegas and *"chinas y criollas"* restaurants remain.

WEST END AVENUE
Between 89th and 90th Streets

Thank goodness for the holdouts—the little Victorians nestled between the great apartment buildings. They allow for badly needed light and air, and add charm to the sophisticated streetscape.

SOLDIER'S AND SAILOR'S MEMORIAL
Riverside Park at 89th Street

I had always been taken with this beautiful monument. I loved to look at it, to caress its lines with my pen. But as I completed the last stroke, I was horrified to discover that it is a monument to the North! (I was born in Virginia.)

90TH STREET
Between West End and Riverside

Oh, it's so intellectual up here! While I drew this, I was invited to join a Buddhist chant group that also discusses the accepted use of common language in advertising.

REDEVELOPMENT VIEW
Amsterdam Avenue and 90th Street, looking northeast

The top and the bottom of the Upper
West Side are gone, victims of "redevelopment."
But when I draw, the pen doesn't show this
"progress": These skyscrapers appear as charming
as their friend, the El Dorado, down the street.

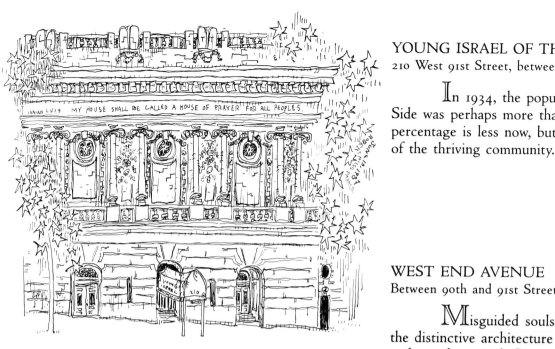

YOUNG ISRAEL OF THE UPPER WEST SIDE
210 West 91st Street, between Amsterdam and Broadway

In 1934, the population of the Upper West Side was perhaps more than half Jewish. That percentage is less now, but Jewish life remains part of the thriving community.

WEST END AVENUE
Between 90th and 91st Streets

Misguided souls think the distinctive architecture ends at about 86th Street. They haven't looked up here, at this Gothic charmer with a Greek accent.

A MEMORIAL FOR CHARLES
91st Street between Central Park West and Columbus

The rooflines along these streets reached harmonious heights atop a happy mixture of building materials and styles. This harmonic potpourri was a romantic idea from the late nineteenth-century; the buildings are a fitting memorial for a man who worked to preserve them.

WHERE STACY LIVES NOW
92nd Street between Central Park West and Columbus

A simple little Victorian one could find anywhere in America: once lots of people called these houses "home." So does Stacy, now.

CENTRAL PARK WEST
Between 93rd and 94th Streets

On this block, Renaissance arches live next door to Egyptian branches. Swartz & Gross, who built the apartment house at 94th Street in 1929, must have designed nearly as many buildings as Emery Roth. But this apartment house is surely their most interesting: papyrus stalks fan out at the top—hints of Aida and the Nile. The motif is most unusual, even in this part of town.

WHERE GENE LIVES
West 93rd Street at Amsterdam

The folk architecture of the 1940s can seem pretty dull compared to earlier buildings on the Upper West Side, but nice compared to what came later.

POMANDER WALK
Between Broadway and West End and 94th and 95th Streets

Pomander Walk is an English stage set come to life, buried in the middle of a city block. The original street, in the London suburb of Chiswick, became the setting (and title) of an early twentieth-century play. The builder Thomas Healy liked the set and in 1922 asked architects King & Campbell to recreate it, this time as a real street in New York. Pomander Walk is a gem of a lane nestled in a forest of huge apartment buildings, with gaily colored shutters and flower-bordered paths.

AN AFTERNOON VIEW
FROM THE CENTRAL PARK RESERVOIR
Central Park at 94th Street, looking west

EARL'S COURT
306 West 94th Street, between West End and Riverside

Although West Side apartment buildings often have names, they are mostly forgotten now. But a careful look over entryways is sometimes rewarding. The Earl's Court—the Earl of what?

140

THE SYMPHONY SPACE BLOCK
Broadway between 94th and 95th Streets

When Thomas Healy built this block, he created an indoor skating rink and shops. Eventually, the rink and shops gave way to two very important Upper West Side establishments—the Thalia, a revival movie house, the little Pomander bookstore, and Symphony Space. Now the Thalia is closed and the shops boarded up, and the bookstore has moved ten blocks further uptown.

227 RIVERSIDE DRIVE
At 95th Street

Like the architecture and people, pets also vary from neighborhood to neighborhood. On elegant Riverside Drive, one sees expensive Chinese wrinkle dogs; on the tougher streets up here, Mexican Chihuahuas.

WEST END AVENUE
Between 95th and 96th Streets

On Friday nights before sundown, the faithful step out and walk past the West End town houses, on their way to temple—the men in black suits speaking Hebrew, the women in fancy dress, often some steps behind. The houses watch this ages-old progression, as they always have.

95TH STREET
At Broadway

Life is a bit more serious up here, not so pretty, with less of the fancy dance you see farther down the avenue.

136–140 WEST 95TH STREET
Between Amsterdam and Columbus

The side streets up here sometimes have the look of charming lanes. The sidewalks have been extended, and the fine old trees create a pleasant place to ramble.

N.Y. FLOWERS & PLANT EXCHANGE
Plant Shed

THE HOLY NAME OF JESUS ROMAN CATHOLIC CHURCH
96th Street and Amsterdam Avenue

What a busy place 96th Street is! The subway stops always set the stage, and on the Upper West Side that stage is always changing. Thus: the newcomers need plants, the old timers, religion. The composite picture is typical of the Upper West Side.

THE ENID
104 West 96th Street, between Columbus and Amsterdam

Another building still proudly showing its name. This time a cleaned-up apartment house, with the typical Upper West Side stoop-loungers. These days, the stoop-lounging phenomenon is more apparent from 96th on up.

THE VIEW FROM DENNIS'S HOUSE AT THE GRAMONT

98th Street and Broadway, looking northwest

They say George Gershwin had his piano hoisted up through his window in that huge building across the way, the White hall. The West Side is a lullaby of such stories.

98TH STREET
At Riverside, looking south to 96th Street

This great sweeping view to the south includes a tip of the hat to the Wild West—the Cliff Dwellers' Apartments.

METRO THEATER
2626 Broadway between 99th and 100th Streets

This 1933 gem of a movie house by Boak & Parts has been gloriously restored. Sporting a Deco-lady in cameo, it is a jewel in the still-grubby Broadway of the 90s.

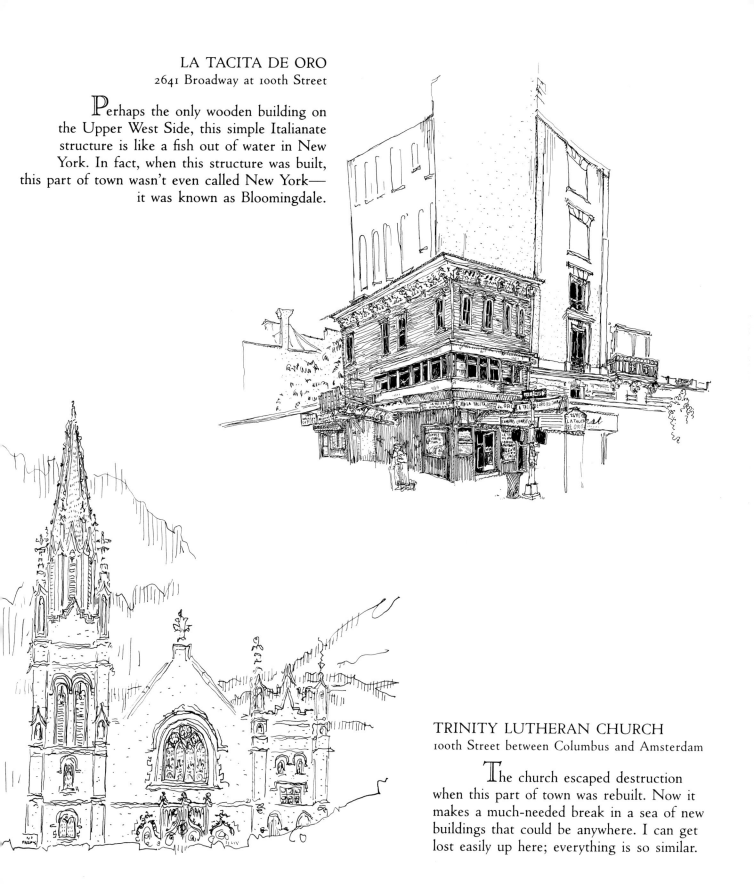

LA TACITA DE ORO
2641 Broadway at 100th Street

Perhaps the only wooden building on the Upper West Side, this simple Italianate structure is like a fish out of water in New York. In fact, when this structure was built, this part of town wasn't even called New York— it was known as Bloomingdale.

TRINITY LUTHERAN CHURCH
100th Street between Columbus and Amsterdam

The church escaped destruction when this part of town was rebuilt. Now it makes a much-needed break in a sea of new buildings that could be anywhere. I can get lost easily up here; everything is so similar.

100TH STREET
At Central Park West

A combination of Beaux-Arts splendor and Latino funk characterizes this neighborhood.

101ST STREET
Between West End and Riverside

This is a view off Riverside looking up 101st. If you looked closely you'd be delighted by carved garlands, perhaps gargoyles, surely faces over the windows and doors. Many were hand-carved, others cast from hand molds.

856 WEST END AVENUE
At 102nd Street

This 1893 Schneider & Herter building dates from a time when West End Avenue was "the" place to live, long before the monster apartment buildings came along.

BROADWAY
Between 103rd and 104th Streets

Service stores fill every single space. But they aren't original: the corner—now occupied by La Cabana, Sloan's, and a law office—was once an automat. The other stores too are new. These businesses probably won't last either, however, as new and fresher merchandise comes along. Change is the rule in New York.

105TH STREET
At Broadway

On the new Upper West Side, beautiful people in their twenties eat endive salad and discuss the joys of conservatism— even at 105th Street!

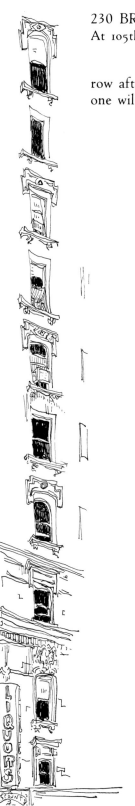

230 BROADWAY
At 105th Street

Sometimes it is irritating to draw row after row of windows; sometimes, just one will suffice.

A LITTLE SCRIBBLE ON RIVERSIDE DRIVE
Between 105th and 106th Streets

French Beaux-Arts town houses form a frothy and sophisticated row. Parisian architecture sneaks in all over the Upper West Side.

THE TOWERS NURSING HOME
2 West 106th Street at Central Park West

There are many towered Romanesque structures in this neighborhood, but the abandoned nursing home may be the most intriguing. The 1887 building was New York's first cancer hospital; architect Charles C. Haight thought the rooms with rounded corners would be easier to clean. This haunting nest of empty windows and crumbling brick may become a backdrop for some other towers: high-rises may be added to realize the value of the land and permit the restoration of the old hospital.

VIEW
Looking down Amsterdam from 106th Street

Up here, in the summertime, the windows are wide open and the people lean out. Neighbors try to drown each other out with the sounds of salsa and rap. Farther south, the windows are often shut, and the sound is more likely Mozart.

THE MANHASSET
301 West 108th Street at Broadway

When people think the "good stuff" is all in the 70s, it's only because they haven't visited up here. The Manhasset, built in 1904 by Janes & Leo, may look a bit shabby, but I'll bet not for long. Even in its tattered state it remains a grand mansarded building. Just wait till it's gussied up.

106TH STREET
At Manhattan Place

The blind, dead architecture is a remnant of the '60s riots. This once-elegant building is now the scene of graffiti and trash.

LUKE AND EMILY'S BUILDING
360 Riverside Drive at 108th Street

West of Broadway, the
upper Upper West Side explodes
with Renaissance Revival apartment
buildings full of serious types—
Columbia faculty and students. The
scurrying people have a distracted,
intellectual look, and the street
vendors sell used copies of Kant,
not *Playboy*. This building was
in the process of a cleanup,
now finished.

COLUMBUS
At 108th Street

We're not quite the sophisticated town we should be. This row has long been deserted, and the space that could house hundreds serves only as a signboard for the mechanics on the street. Great buildings as a backdrop for a mechanic's shop—a sad commentary in a city with thousands of homeless people.

THE LAST STOP ON THE UPPER WEST SIDE
110th Street and Broadway

Here is a building that could be anywhere in America. The storefront is boarded up, and you'll have to get your donuts somewhere else.

The artist would like to thank the following collectors, who graciously allowed their drawings to be included in this book:

John Austin, Williamsburg, Virginia; Carol Baer, New York, New York; Dr. & Mrs. John Barlow, Rochester, New York; Barbara Barrie, New York; Bob Benites, San Diego, California; Carroll Benter, San Francisco, California; Beverly Boyle, New York; Tommy & Devora Bratton, La Honda, California; Carol Brener, New York; Mosette Broderick, New York; Edward J. Brown, New York; Jenifer Buchanan, New York; Nickie Chaisson, San Diego; Ida Louise Cheney, El Caton, California; Sandra Ciullo, New York; Patrica Clark, Frankfurt, Germany; Geoffrey Colvin, New York; Louisa Craddack, New York; Dale Craig, San Diego; Sharon Crosby, Leucadia, California; Liz Cusick, Baltimore, Maryland; Gary Donner, New York; Phil Durkem, Swinson, Wiltshire, England; Harry Evans, San Diego; John Evertse, La Mesa, California; Dr. Richard Friedman, San Diego; Jack Germain, New York; Keith Gilbert, New York; Rose Gilbert, Lakeside, California; Peggy Glenn, Scottsdale, Arizona; Merika Gopaul, San Diego; Robert Grabowski, New York; Hugh Grambau, Washington, D.C.; Bill Hanes, New York; George Haverstick, San Diego; Nancy Hayward, San Diego; Artie Herman, New York; John Lawrence Hiduchick III, San Diego; Sally Hoover, Phoenix, Arizona; Leo Kirchhoff, Zomba, Malawi; Jon Lach, Hoboken, New Jersey; Margaret Liebling, New York; Phyllis & Joe Lisanti, New York; Bertie Lovell, San Diego; Nancy & Larna MacHutchin, La Jolla, California; Dale Manicum, San Diego; Veronica McGowan, El Cajon, California; Ruth McMichaels, Leucadia; Paul McNally, Palm Springs, California; Clark Mires, El Cajon; Dr. & Mrs. Don Mitchell, San Diego; Ann Morrison, Port Washington, New York; Dr. & Mrs. Robert Neveln, San Diego; Kate Numlist, New York; Stacy Osur, New York; Penny Pergament, Phoenix; Alfred Pigano, San Diego; Gary Rees, San Diego, California; Rich Romo, San Diego; Sally Scarsfield, Hoboken; James Shaver, Pacific Palisades, California; Arlene, Bruce, Charles, Douglas, and Rachel Simon; Valerie Smith, Princeton, New Jersey; Renée Stauffer, Los Angeles, California; Mary Parker Stuart, Norfolk, Virginia; Daniel Talbot, New York; Sue Taylor, San Diego; Michael Teaford, Asheville, North Carolina; Pat Tidmore, San Francisco; Susan Tolzman, Green Mountain Falls, Colorado; David Van Leer, Davis, California; Liz Waldorf, New York, New York; Randy Wallace, La Jolla; Dr. Harvey Werblood, New York; Anthony C. Wood, New York.

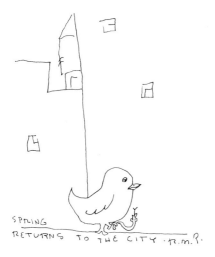

SPRING
RETURNS TO THE CITY · R.m.P.

BIBLIOGRAPHY

Andrews, Wayne. *Architecture in New York, a Photographic History*. New York: Atheneum, 1969.

Berrol, Selma. "Manhattan's Jewish West Side." *New York Affairs* 10, i (Winter 1987): 13–32.

Birmingham, Stephen. *Life at the Dakota: New York's Most Unusual Address*. New York: Random House, 1979.

Blumenson, John J.-G. *Identifying American Architecture: a Pictorial Guide to Styles and Terms, 1600–1945*, second edition, revised and enlarged. Nashville: American Association for State and Local History, 1981.

Federal Writers' Project of the Works Progress Administration in New York City. *New York Panorama, a Companion to the WPA Guide to New York City*. 1938; reprinted New York: Pantheon Books, 1984.

———. *The WPA Guide to New York City: the Federal Writers' Project Guide to 1930s New York*. 1939; reprinted New York: Pantheon Books, 1984.

Goldberger, Paul. *The City Observed: New York; a Guide to the Architecture of Manhattan*. New York: Random House, 1979.

Jacoby, Stephen M. *Architectural Sculpture in New York City*. New York: Dover Publications, 1975.

Trager, James. *West of Fifth: The Rise and Fall and Rise of Manhattan's West Side*. New York: Atheneum, 1987.

Watson, Edward B. *New York Then and Now: 83 Manhattan Sites Photographed in the Past and in the Present*. New York: Dover Publications, 1976.

White, Norval and Elliot Willensky. *AIA Guide to New York City*, revised edition. New York: Collier Books, 1978.

Wolfe, Gerard R. *New York, a Guide to the Metropolis: Walking Tours of Architecture and History*. New York: New York University Press, 1975.

Wright, Carol von Pressentin. *New York, Blue Guide series*. New York: W. W. Norton, 1983.